GREATER MEKONG SUBREGION COVID-19 RESPONSE AND RECOVERY PLAN 2021–2023

SEPTEMBER 2021

ADB

Contents

Abbreviations

ADB	Asian Development Bank
COVID-19	coronavirus disease
GDP	gross domestic product
GMS	Greater Mekong Subregion
Lao PDR	Lao People's Democratic Republic
RCI	regional cooperation and integration

Executive Summary

The Greater Mekong Subregion (GMS) has been relatively successful in controlling the spread of the coronavirus disease (COVID-19). The social protection, economic stimulus, and business support programs that have been put in place have proved to be instrumental in limiting the number of people falling below the poverty line. However, the pandemic has a significant adverse impact on the economic and social fabric of the subregion. The purpose of the GMS COVID-19 Response and Recovery Plan 2021–2023 (the Plan) is to coordinate the efforts of GMS countries on issues that require greater regional cooperation and integration (RCI) to more effectively respond to the COVID-19 pandemic.

The immediate needs of the subregion are to control the number of COVID-19 infections and related deaths, expand and accelerate vaccination programs, ensure the continued growth of economies, and reduce the impacts on the poor and vulnerable. In the medium term, focus will rest on rebuilding economies and people's livelihoods. The Plan will support the subregion's economy during the COVID-19 pandemic, facilitating economic recovery and helping prepare the GMS for any further crises.

The Plan identifies a limited number of achievable initiatives across the subregion within the medium term. It complements and supports implementation of the GMS Economic Cooperation Program Strategic Framework 2030 (GMS-2030) as well as commitments of GMS countries under the Sustainable Development Goals and the National Determined Contributions to the United Nations Framework Convention on Climate Change. The Plan supplements national COVID-19 responses by focusing on RCI priorities. It will (i) balance health, economic, environmental, and social priorities; (ii) ensure private sector involvement; (iii) engage local governments and communities; and (iv) be widely and effectively communicated.

The Plan has three pillars:

- **Pillar 1** protects lives with a One Health approach to ensure the health not only of people but also of animals, crops and food products, and urban environments.

- **Pillar 2** protects the vulnerable and poor by offering them opportunities in border areas and GMS economic corridors, as well as supporting the safe and orderly movement of labor.

- **Pillar 3** ensures that borders remain open to (i) accelerate inclusive, green, and resilient economic activity; (ii) facilitate transport and trade; (iii) rebuild agriculture; and (iv) generate safe and seamless tourism opportunities.

The implementation of the Plan is the responsibility of the senior officials of the GMS Program and GMS sector working groups, supported by the GMS Secretariat. Private sector organizations and GMS knowledge centers will assist in refining and implementing the initiatives and activities.

I.   Purpose

1.   The Greater Mekong Subregion (GMS) is an increasingly integrated economic and social subregion. The intraregional movement of people, trade in goods and services, and sharing of regional public goods has increased significantly since the establishment of the GMS Program in 1992. While the health impact of the coronavirus disease (COVID-19) has been contained to some extent, the adverse economic impact in the GMS has been quite severe. The purpose of the COVID-19 Response and Recovery Plan (the Plan) is to coordinate the efforts of GMS member countries on issues that require greater regional cooperation and integration (RCI) in response to the COVID-19 pandemic, and to support the subregion during the recovery phase. This Plan complements and supports the implementation of the GMS Economic Cooperation Program Strategic Framework 2030 (GMS-2030).

2.   The Plan will also help identify priority projects to accelerate the subregion's response and recovery (Appendix). The Plan is a living document that will be monitored and adjusted as GMS countries recover from the social and economic impacts of COVID-19.

An integrated subregion. There are many international border crossings between countries of the Greater Mekong Subregion where goods and people cross every day. (left) Cross-border traffic at Lao Cai between Viet Nam and the People's Republic of China. (below) Aerial view of the border check point in Savanakhet, Lao PDR near the Second Thai–Lao Friendship Bridge.

II.   COVID-19 Impact

3.   As COVID-19 spread across the GMS in early 2020, a call by GMS governments to lock down their borders proved successful in curtailing the transmission of the virus. Yet, more than a million (1,088,923) had contracted the disease and 16,003 have died.[1] The lockdowns affected the flow of trade, investment, and tourism. The closure of local businesses, schools, and venues of mass gatherings also had a serious economic impact on households and businesses, placing significant fiscal pressure on GMS governments.

4.   Across the GMS, the gross domestic product (GDP) posted a small growth of 0.2% in 2020 compared to 2019 before rebounding to 6.1% growth in 2021.[2] While promising, there are considerable risks in the subregion achieving continued recovery. Total GMS merchandise exports declined by 60% in 2020 compared to the previous year, reflecting weak external demand for GMS goods and services as advanced economies continued to contract. In the tourism sector, international arrivals fell by about 80% across the subregion in 2020, suppressing demand through the entire tourism value chain.

COVID-19 and international travel. Empty airports and airplanes have become the norm because of travel restrictions imposed by countries during the COVID-19 pandemic.

[1]   World Health Organization. Corona Virus Disease Dashboard. https://covid19.who.int/ (accessed 1 August 2021); John Hopkins University. COVID-19 Map. https://coronavirus.jhu.edu/map.html (accessed 1 August 2021); and United Nations Population Fund. World Population Dashboard. https://www.unfpa.org/data/world-population-dashboard (accessed 19 February 2021).

[2]   ADB estimates based on ADB. 2021. *Asian Development Outlook* (ADO) Supplement: Renewed Outbreaks and Divergent Recoveries. *July.* Manila. https://www.adb.org/publications/ado-supplement-july-2021

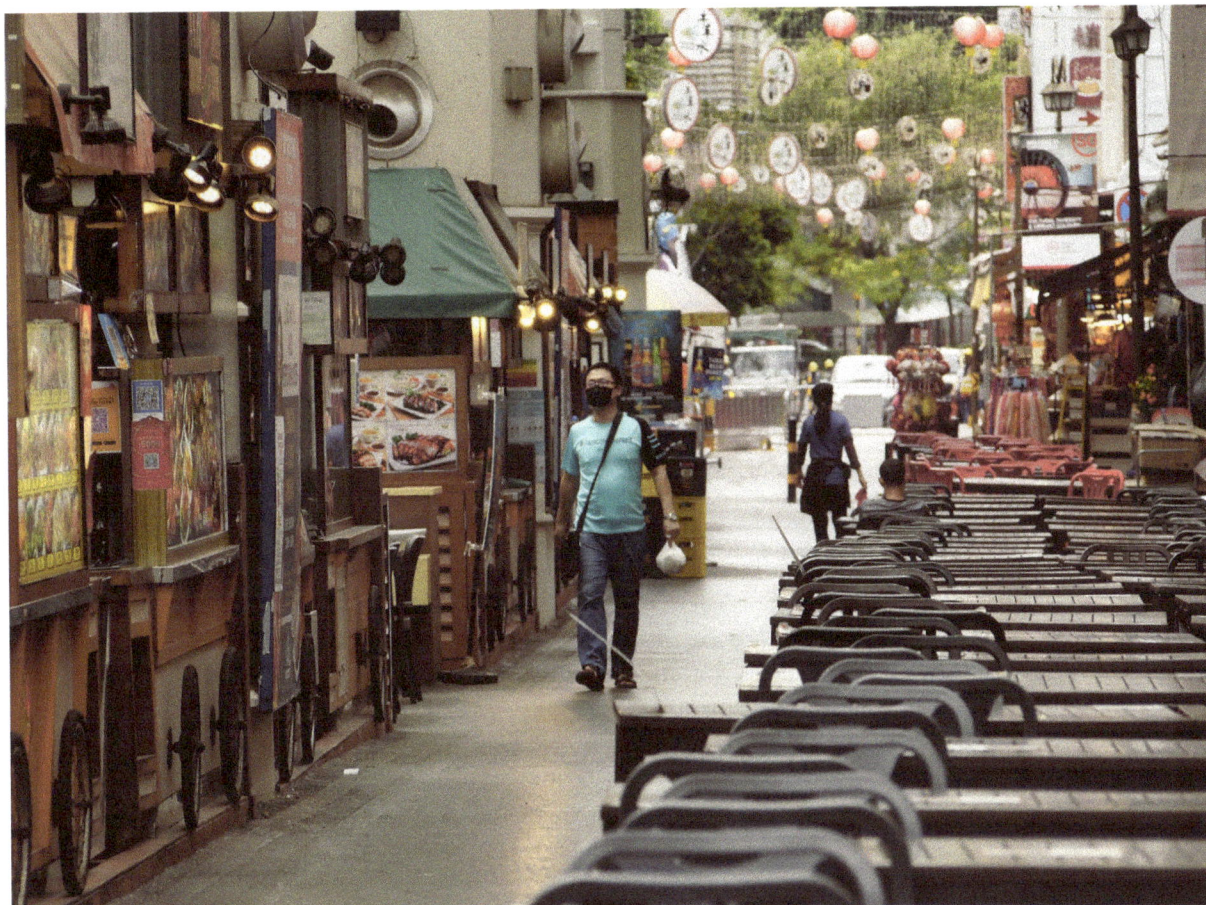

The effects of lockdown on businesses. The crowds are sparse in normally busy shops and restaurants because of the COVID-19 pandemic.

5.   Across the GMS, approximately 7 million people became unemployed by mid-2020, an estimate that would be substantially higher were it to include the informal economy and those involved in the agricultural sector. A further 8 million people have been thrust below the poverty line.[3] It is estimated that more than 340,000 migrant workers have been forced to return home, many of whom have neither housing, land for subsistence living, nor alternative income.

6.   Despite the differences between the GMS economies and their stages of development, there are some common patterns with respect to the COVID-19 impact across the subregion. GMS countries now suffer a decrease in global demand for their goods and services; serious disruptions in regional and global supply chain; and increased difficulties in transporting traded goods across borders due to COVID-19-related concerns. Domestically, these factors have resulted in the closure of businesses, constrained access to international finance, a large number of business failures, higher unemployment and poverty, and significant stress on social protection systems in many GMS countries. In dealing with these challenges, various GMS governments continue to struggle to maintain a prudent fiscal stance given the severe revenue compression and significantly higher expenditure requirements.

---

[3]   Data from various sources including: International Labour Organization. 2021. *World Employment and Social Outlook: Trends 2021.* Switzerland; International Labour Organization. 2021. *TRIANGLE in ASEAN Briefing Notes.* Thailand; and Asian Development Bank Institute, Organisation for Economic Co-operation and Development, and International Labour Organization. 2021. *Labor Migration in Asia: Impacts of the COVID-19 Crisis and the Post-Pandemic Future.*

III. Greater Mekong Subregion National Recovery Plans

7.   There is a particular commonality in the response of GMS countries to the impact of COVID-19, and in the protection of their citizens and economic base. For households, these include provision of (i) cash relief to families and wage support to workers, (ii) special support programs for poor and returning migrants, (iii) financial support to those with COVID–19 (in some countries only), and (iv) relief to cover utility and transport costs.

8.   In protecting the economic base, GMS countries have focused on micro, small, and medium-sized enterprises (MSMEs), as well as state-owned enterprises. These measures have included (i) provision of specific tax and/or duty relief and/or holidays to firms, (ii) concessional financing for businesses, and (iii) reduction of interest rates and reserve requirements by central banks so that commercial banks can pass on these benefits.

9.   Along with protecting their economies, governments have also significantly expanded health care spending, including for those directly affected by COVID–19; focused attention on education by developing online schooling modalities where required; and reduced nonessential government expenditures to create fiscal space for all their additional needs.

10.   GMS countries are now developing medium-term recovery plans (2021–2023) aimed at rebuilding their local economies and rejuvenating regional and global value chains. The overall GMS Program is well-suited to address several of the constraints encountered in building the RCI momentum back, in coordination with national medium-term recovery plans.

Focus on supporting micro, small, and medium-sized enterprises (MSMEs). Many MSMEs such as boat operators transporting visitors to tourist areas are hard hit by the COVID-19 pandemic.

IV. Response and Recovery Plan for COVID-19

11. **Rationale.** The immediate needs of the subregion are to protect the health and well-being of the populations in a volatile environment by controlling COVID-19 infections and deaths, and to reduce the impacts on the poor and vulnerable. In the medium term, focus will be on rebuilding the economies and moving people out of poverty in a sustained manner. This also implies (i) preparing the GMS against further pandemic surges with efficient testing and treatment methods, (ii) securing and distributing COVID-19 vaccines and implementing vaccination drives across the subregion, and (iii) providing policy and financial support for post-pandemic recovery.

12. While sound and effective national policies are essential, they alone may not be sufficient to defeat the pandemic. For a successful GMS economic recovery, supplementary efforts to promote greater regional cooperation are key to further leverage reforms at the national level to ensure a more sustained, inclusive, green, resilient, and stronger recovery. The GMS Program, with its project-based and practical approach, as well as its robust institutional framework, is well positioned to coordinate a subregion-wide response in several key areas. A multisector and multi-thematic plan is critical for GMS Program efforts.

13. **Objectives.** The Plan identifies areas and initiatives for common action, applying the comparative advantages found within the GMS Program. The Plan's objectives are to (i) support the subregion's citizens and economies during the COVID-19 pandemic, and ensure health for all; (ii) facilitate the region's economic recovery so that it becomes stronger, greener, more resilient, and able to better protect the poor and vulnerable; and (iii) reduce the adverse risks and impacts of future crises to the GMS.

14. **Principles.** Four principles underpin the delivery of the Plan, including: (i) flexibility and adaptability in responding to new challenges and utilizing scientific and people-centered COVID-19 response; (ii) good balance between health, economic, and social objectives; (iii) effective communication and involvement of local

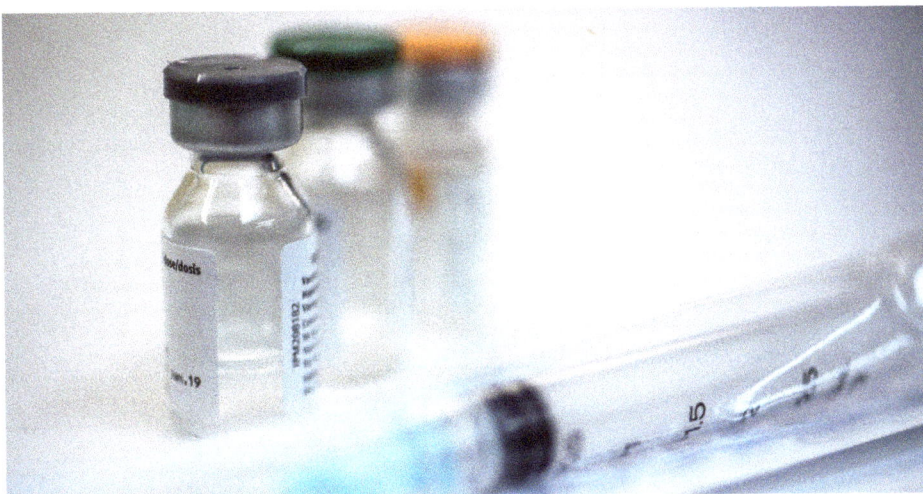

Rebuilding economies. Securing and distributing COVID-19 vaccines are immediate responses of the Greater Mekong Subregion governments.

Leveraging resources. (above) Accessing, leveraging, and coordinating the significant resources needed to respond to the pandemic is essential.

Balancing health, economic, and social objectives. (right) A medical worker wears personal protective equipment in a COVID-19 testing laboratory.

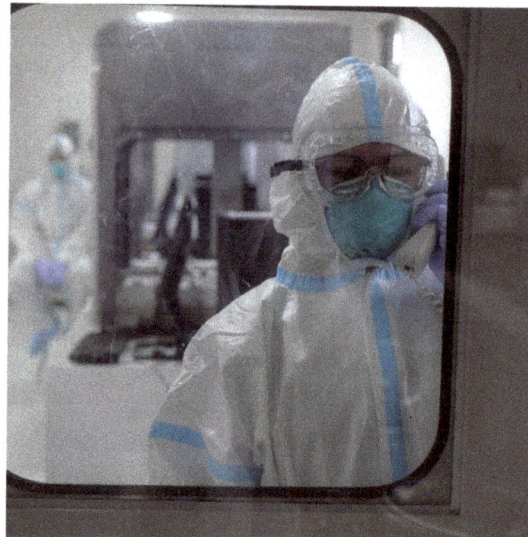

governments, communities, and the private sector; and (iv) ability to leverage development partners, and domestic and private sector resources to achieve all the initiatives and targets under the Plan.

15. **Flexibility and adaptability.** The principles, approaches, and crosscutting issues of the GMS-2030 are equally applicable to the implementation of the Plan. The Plan complements and supports the GMS-2030 and reinforces national COVID-19 response plans to leverage domestic development through regional integration and mutual support. The responses in the COVID-19 Plan should be people-centered and science-based. To achieve this, the Plan needs to remain flexible and adaptable to respond to new challenges during its implementation.

16. **Balancing health, economic, and social objectives.** The immediate needs are to ensure people's health and assist the most vulnerable. The medium-term response includes ensuring ongoing health and safety while rebuilding economic activity, including trade and tourism; and also maintaining environmental resilience. Building resilience requires developing health as well as sanitary and phytosanitary systems to protect society. In addition to achieving a good balance between these objectives, there also needs to be balance between the immediate response measures, medium-term recovery, and longer-term focus on resilience.

17. **Effective communication.** The involvement of local governments, communities, and the private sector is essential. The importance of collaboration across borders and the need to involve a wider range of diverse stakeholders from central, state/provincial, and local governments, the private sector, academia, civil society, and development partners has been further highlighted by the COVID-19 pandemic. Many activities under the Plan require the active participation of multiple stakeholders. This will require efficient communication to them and the public on the objectives, activities and benefits of the Plan, as well as close consultation during its implementation.

18. **Leveraging resources.** The resources needed to respond to and recover from COVID-19 are quite significant, and include finance, technology, and knowledge, on top of the critical human resources. Accessing, leveraging, and coordinating these resources to maximize their impact is essential. As GMS governments contribute significant new resources, development partners' initiatives to support government plans are getting underway, including those focused on regional cooperation. The private sector is playing an increasingly important role in identifying and addressing its own recovery needs and helping to implement government plans. Regional and global knowledge institutions are providing plenty of materials upon which to base plans and implementation approaches. The GMS sector working groups, task forces, and the GMS Secretariat will continue to play a critical role in leveraging these resources.

V.   Pillars of the Plan

19.   The Plan will be delivered through three thematic pillars to ensure clarity of purpose and action across sectors. These pillars target the critical constraints experienced or anticipated in relation to RCI during the response and recovery phases. They also enable sector-specific actions to take place through sector working groups, ensuring the determined and coordinated action between these groups. Pillar 1 aims to protect lives with a One Health approach to ensure the health not only of people but also of animals, crops and food products, and urban environments. Pillar 2 protects the vulnerable and poor by offering them opportunities in border areas and along GMS economic corridors, as well as supporting the safe and orderly movement of labor. Pillar 3 ensures that borders remain open to accelerate inclusive, green, and resilient economic activity; facilitate transport and trade; rebuild agriculture; and generate safe and seamless tourism opportunities.

Pillar 1 – Protecting Lives—A One Health Approach

20.   **Healthy people.** GMS countries have been effective in responding to the threat of COVID–19. They have kept cases at relatively low numbers while ensuring the continued delivery of much-needed health services for both COVID-19 and non-COVID-19 cases, including those with non-communicable diseases. Despite these efforts, the subregion remains susceptible to a surge in new infections, witnessed globally, as governments have reduced restrictions and reopened borders. The emergence of new strains of the virus is also posing new challenges to the subregion. Therefore, there is urgent need to scale-up testing, tracing, and roll-out of vaccines to ensure full economic recovery in the subregion.[4]

21.   Health cooperation leadership, and intraregional capacity building are core to the effective stewardship of the subregion's response to public health threats like COVID-19. Ensuring timely access to a safe and effective

A One Health Approach.
The approach will strengthen health systems with an emphasis on the health care workforce located along borders.

---

[4]   https://www.cnbc.com/2021/06/16/covid-imf-chief-says-vaccine-policy-is-the-most-important-economic-driver.html (accessed in July 2021).

COVID-19 vaccine is a key element for cooperation. Large gaps in capacity for vaccine manufacturing, as well as regulatory capacity for medical products, exist between GMS countries. Financial and technical resources for vaccine sourcing, procurement, distribution, and delivery are a further constraint. The multilateral development banks, including ADB and others, shall continue to play a vital role in providing financial support to the subregion's countries for purchasing vaccines, on the basis of their preference. While GMS countries have vaccine distribution networks for regular immunization programs, these may not be adequate for the COVID-19 vaccine. Further support for vaccine procurement, capacity building in the regulation of vaccines, supply-chain assessment and upgrading, and the development of risk communication and vaccine delivery strategies will be prioritized under this Plan. GMS countries will strengthen cooperation on vaccines to ensure that accessible and affordable COVID-19 vaccines are available for people in the subregion. The GMS Program will facilitate country dialogue to better comprehend the needs and gaps for vaccines in each GMS country and promote regional mechanisms for pooled procurement and subregional logistics and supply chain. This aims to achieve timely access and better negotiating power with major manufacturers and efficient distribution of procured vaccines.

22.   A One Health response to public health threats reinforces multisector cooperation as a building block for effective response to COVID-19. Developing institutional mechanisms and capacities for a One Health approach within the subregion will set the foundation for effective prevention and containment of future pandemic threats. While developing a multisector, coordinated approach is an ongoing effort in the subregion, a good foundation has been laid in the GMS countries' early responses to COVID-19, which will provide lessons for strengthening collaboration further. In responding to this threat, GMS countries will be guided by the regional health actions agreed under the GMS Health Cooperation Strategy 2019–2023.

23.   Health systems will be strengthened with an emphasis on the cross-border health services in locations along borders where migrant populations pass through and reside. Border area health systems are critical to COVID-19 response when and as countries move to reopen borders. Investment in infrastructure at points-of-entry, in health facilities for sanitation and hygiene, in testing, and in isolation and quarantine facilities will be promoted to facilitate the safe movement of people. Investment in digital health technologies, such as electronic personal health records that link the health information in departure and destination countries, will be prioritized. Collaboration with the private sector in the provision of protective medical equipment, as well as vaccine research, production, and distribution will also be promoted. GMS countries and development partners will support projects that aim to respond to the unique challenges posed by COVID-19, such as increased vulnerability among people with chronic non-communicable diseases in border areas and among cross-border migrant populations.

24.   Strengthening core health regulation capacities within the public health systems will provide the foundation for robust national and subregional health systems with the capacity to prevent, detect, and respond to transnational health threats. With support from development partners, GMS countries will strengthen their collaborative and coordinated COVID-19 response by:

(i)   enhancing national laboratory systems and collaboration among them for rapid and accurate diagnostics;

(ii)   improving national and GMS-wide surveillance systems for the timely detection of cases and effective contact tracing; and

(iii)   building the capacity and collaboration of national health systems to communicate risk, prevent and control infection, and coordinate and operate during an emergency.

25.   **Healthy animals, crops, and food products.** This can be achieved through harmonized quality and safety platforms. COVID-19 prevention measures, such as lockdowns, travel restrictions, and border controls, have had negative consequences for the agri-food sector, including but not limited to:

(i) the difficulty of moving live animals and agri-food products to markets across borders,

(ii) restrictions that may limit seasonal border crossings,

(iii) reduced capacity to purchase necessary production inputs, and

(iv) restricted access to labor and professional services.

26.   These challenges have led to a decrease in processing capacity for agri-food products, as well as a loss of sales and a slowdown of market activity. COVID-19 may also have undermined the capacity of some GMS countries to prevent and control transboundary animal diseases.

27.   The GMS is particularly prone to an increase in health risks from the rising volumes of informal trade in livestock and food products, as well as wildlife caught and then traded in live markets and consumed in GMS countries. This increases the likelihood of a spillover of disease-causing agents from wildlife to livestock and/or humans. Demand for safe and quality food by urban populations and tourists is growing in all GMS countries. The subregion still faces several challenges, however, including:

(i) the lack of harmonized safety and quality assurance systems,

(ii) ineffective control of transboundary animal diseases and zoonoses, and

(iii) antimicrobial resistance that constrains the GMS potential for agri-food exports.

28.   Support for sanitary and phytosanitary measures to facilitate GMS trade has increased the technical capacity for surveillance and inspection, helping to ensure plant and animal health as well as food safety. However, much remains to be done to promote cross-border cooperation and the harmonization of sanitary and phytosanitary measures, standards, and practices.

29.   In response to COVID-19, the GMS Program will invest in livestock disease monitoring and preparedness as well as in healthy livestock value chains in selected countries to reduce the risk of emerging infectious diseases with pandemic potential. Such investments will be in infrastructure, capacity building, and enabling policies. GMS countries will establish disease control zones in priority border areas and address critical infrastructure gaps in livestock health systems and value chains. This includes the remodeling and improvement of laboratories and zoonotic disease and antimicrobial resistance control facilities. Training will be undertaken in:

(i) agri-food product safety and quality, including biosafety and biosecurity measures;

(ii) food safety risk communication, quality assurance, and traceability systems; and

(iii) control of transboundary animal diseases and antimicrobial resistance.

30.   Investments in digital technologies will also be promoted to boost the competitiveness of agri-food value chains in the GMS. These could include reusable reticular cattle identification systems and the Internet of Things for livestock traceability and disease monitoring; and other technology-based livestock epidemic prevention platforms. Along with these investments in infrastructure and technology, the Plan will promote critical enabling policies to mobilize more private sector investments in COVID-19 recovery plans.

31.   The GMS Sustainable Agriculture and Food Security Program (2020–2025) will play a catalytic role in implementing the Plan by conducting:

(i) surveys on RCI with regard to COVID-19 response and recovery efforts, food safety, and quality assurance systems;

(ii) surveys on digital technologies to enhance the competitiveness of agri-food value chains in GMS;

(iii) study visits between GMS and South Asia on climate-smart and COVID-19-responsive agriculture supply-chain management; and

(iv) digital technology demonstrations on green and COVID-19-responsive agribusiness supply chains.

32.   The GMS Program will also prepare knowledge products on inter-subregional cooperation on RCI and mobilization of private sector investments in COVID-19-responsive agribusiness in the GMS

33.   **Healthy city environments.** Cities are the most high-risk environments for the transmission of COVID-19. The population density, common water and sanitation systems, urban transport systems, and large workforces all increase the risk of disease transmission. Cultural norms can also challenge social distancing and transmission reduction efforts. Border cities are even more at risk as they house returning migrants and have a relatively higher concentration of people and goods moving across borders. Efforts to contain community transmission are further hampered by the poor and vulnerable in the border cities, that are unable to cease economic efforts due to inadequate or nonexistent social safety nets.

34.   To address the high-risk elements, the Plan (i) promotes hygiene services, such as setting up handwashing stations in public spaces and providing water supply in urban areas with nonexistent basic infrastructure; (ii) provides financial and technical support to utilities struggling with loss of revenue, reduced availability of critical materials, and deferred investments; (iii) reduces the risk of taking public transport through enhanced social distancing measures, fleet sanitation, enforcement of safety protocols in informal modes of transport, and management of commuters' expectations; and (iv) helps communities maintain social distance in public spaces.

35.   To address the medium-term risks and strengthen infrastructure to build urban reliance, the Plan will:

(i)   improve responses to pandemic situations, especially in terms of planning systems and service delivery, through the enhanced use of digital technologies;

(ii) minimize the spread of disease by creating healthy environments through efficient water sanitation and waste management;

(iii) work toward a whole-of-city approach to solid waste management to ensure real change and protection; and

(iv) identify and implement alternative urban travel options and patterns (e.g., nonmotorized transport, e-vehicles, etc.) and investments in cycling and walking spaces.

36.   Financial sustainability will be important, and city authorities should seek to mobilize diverse innovative green and blue financing options and build valuable partnerships with the private sector. To do this under the Plan, the GMS Program will make use of the ASEAN Catalytic Green Finance Facility under the ASEAN Infrastructure Fund, the Urban Climate Resilience Trust Fund, and the ASEAN Smart Cities Initiative, all managed by the Asian Development Bank (ADB).

Pillar 2 – Protecting the Vulnerable and Poor

37.   **Protect and enhance opportunities to the poor and vulnerable in border areas and GMS economic corridors.** COVID-19 has severely affected businesses and people in border areas and along economic corridors that are highly linked to cross-border trade, investment, and tourism. The pandemic has placed immense stress on these communities, increasing poverty levels and affecting the most vulnerable in particular.

38.   The Plan will accelerate the implementation of Sustainable Development Goals 1, 2, 13, and 17 focusing on poverty alleviation. It will promote the development of border areas as well as collaboration across GMS borders to

facilitate the recovery of these local economies. Supporting the poor and vulnerable will be done through projects under the Plan with a specific focus on this group. Along the economic corridors, economic recovery plans will also target the poor. Projects include upgrading transport linkages, developing the agriculture supply chains, and supporting the recovery of MSMEs. Programs will also continue supporting the health, safety, and finances of poor local households.

39.   **Safe and orderly labor movement and management.** Migrant workers are an essential part of the economies in the GMS, with Thailand alone hosting 3 million migrant workers, mostly from other GMS countries. Many of these migrants had to leave Thailand under COVID-19 lockdowns, affecting the Thai economy as well as the lives of the migrants and their families. Remittances sent by migrant workers are essential for the economies of several GMS countries. In the Lao People's Democratic Republic (Lao PDR), 12% of households receive international remittances; in Cambodia 9%; in Myanmar 7%; and in Viet Nam 4.6%. Remittances could fall by 18% in Viet Nam and Myanmar; 16% in the Lao PDR and Thailand; and 15% in Cambodia.[5] As remittance-dependent households are at high risk of falling into poverty, GMS countries must work together under the Plan to support migrant workers and the households affected while economies recover.

40.   As an initial response to the impacts of COVID-19, GMS countries have begun providing social welfare support to those in poverty or near-poverty. Access to health care and housing has also been given. Where migrant workers are unable to return home, GMS countries will work together to expand support to stranded migrant workers, including upgrading their skills and tapping the skilled workers to help local communities. Stranded migrants will also be given the necessary humanitarian support such as health care and shelter, according to local conditions and regulations.

41.   Social welfare support to migrants must be maintained across the subregion until economies recover sufficiently and labor demand returns to pre-pandemic levels. Continued access to housing and health care will remain important to reverse the rise in poverty and to reduce the risk of this cohort spreading COVID-19. As migrant workers return to work, the GMS Program will promote regional cooperation to facilitate the convenient and safe renewal of working permits and to create a supportive business environment in which to employ migrant workers. GMS countries will work together in developing the regulations for digital platforms used to send and

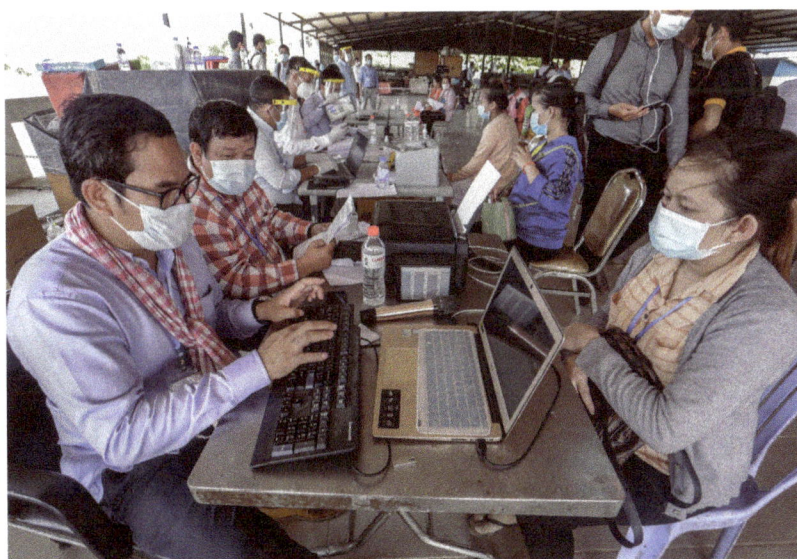

Safe and orderly labor movement and management. Garment migrant workers wait to be checked at the Cambodian border.

---

5   ADB. 2020. *COVID-19 Impact on International Migration, Remittances, and Recipient Households in Developing Asia.* ADB Brief. Manila. https://www.adb.org/sites/default/files/publication/622796/covid-19-impact-migration-remittances-asia.pdf.

receive remittances. GMS governments will also work with the industry to facilitate online job-matching services for overseas workers.

42.   Labor migration support will (i) foster improved migration planning and worker empowerment in preparation for their return to work, (ii) provide the knowledge support for evidence-based migration policy making, (iii) promote coordination between government and employers for the provision and portability of social protection measures in countries of work and countries of origin, (iv) promote skills development and job placement in their home countries to returning migrants, and (v) ensure intraregional labor mobility is gender-responsive and fuels economic recovery in communities of origin and countries of work.

Pillar 3 – Keeping Borders Open and Accelerating Inclusive Economic Activity

43.   **Improved transport and trade facilitation.** The pandemic has severely affected GMS economies by disrupting the flow of goods and services in the subregion's global value chains, thus reducing trade significantly. RCI efforts through the GMS Program are essential to reopen borders to trade. A prerequisite for reopening the borders will be the effective enforcement of health, safety, and security requirements for the COVID-19 pandemic and balancing these against the benefits of trade. The real gains to transport and trade facilitation can be achieved through coordinated and collaborative reforms at the borders. Five areas have been identified to help facilitate transport and trade within the subregion while addressing the longer-term viability of the "Early Harvest" implementation of the Cross-Border Transport and Trade Facilitation in the Greater Mekong Subregion.

44.   **First, increased transparency and improved notification.** GMS countries will inform each other of the current border controls in place due to COVID-19—temporary closures, revised customs clearance processes, and immigration and quarantine requirements—as well as any changes to these controls before they are implemented to reduce the risk of the traded goods failing to cross the border or of unnecessary delays caused by insufficient preparations for epidemic control requirements and cross-border customs clearance. This communication should be formalized through the National Transport Facilitation Committee focal points of each GMS country.

45.   **Second, improved communication.** Rapid communication platforms between National Transport Facilitation Committee focal points will be established to compile and share other transport and trade facilitation procedures. Public health information will also be developed. This could be extended to a single national and regional portal to facilitate the flow of information within the industry.

46.   **Third, coordinated back-to-normal planning.** Each GMS country will develop a national back-to-normal transport and trade facilitation action plan, subdivided into specific phases, with criteria for progression to each successive phase. The plan will cover goods transport, group passenger transport, and private transport, coordinated with non-road transport modes and relevant agencies such as health and tourism. Discussions and negotiations of coordinated cross-border reopening is best undertaken on a subregional basis and/or in country pairs. The plan will include actions to facilitate such a coordinated approach.

47.   **Fourth, enhance communication and integration of changes in border arrangements.** These reforms will only be as effective as the industries' understanding of the changes and their capacity to apply them. Meetings with private sector operators will be organized to keep everyone informed and to develop new initiatives on communication, information dissemination, and trailer-swap and back-to-normal planning. Highlighting the importance of cross-border transport and trade will assist with compliance of COVID-19-related controls and limit COVID-19 transmission; hence, it is imperative that the public understands the measures being undertaken concerning this.

48. **Fifth, enhance cooperation to ensure the smooth flow of goods.** The role of trade facilitation is crucial in ensuring the trade of essential goods. Strengthening cooperation among customs agencies in the GMS will contribute to expediting the clearance of goods at the entry points of land, air, and seaports without compromising countries' safety requirements, standards, and quality for those essential goods. Such cooperation would include, among others:

(i)   the adoption of interim transit arrangement along the GMS economic corridors, at least for the GMS transport permit holders;

(ii) border agency cooperation to facilitate the import of critical supplies; and

(iii) intensified knowledge and experience-sharing on best practices in trade facilitation.

49. Customs modernization in GMS countries would also be intensified, such as:

(i)   further development of national single windows; and

(ii) enhanced risk management to prioritize the clearance of imports and exports of low-risk critical supplies, which will enable the possible relaxation of procedural formalities at the border.

50. Tightening cooperation under regional free trade arrangements will help GMS economies address tariff and nontariff barriers, facilitate, and promote the free flow of goods and services, enhance two-way investment, and maintain the integrity of supply chains during the post COVID-19 era. The implementation of the recently signed Regional Comprehensive Economic Partnership Agreement (RCEP) in the GMS will require dedicated support to harness the benefits of the Partnership. GMS countries will work together, with the support of development partners, to adapt and adjust to this and other free trade agreements. They can do this by analyzing the new agreements and their benefits to the GMS, preparing to implement these agreements, and capturing the benefits of the new RCEP, expediting domestic ratification processes to facilitate the early entry into force of the RCEP.

51. **Rebuilding agricultural trade.** COVID-19 has increased food security risks, reduced food consumption and nutrition, and affected jobs, particularly across the informal sector. Longer lockdowns and shortages of labor have reduced the scale of crop production and disrupted logistics chains. GMS countries in a post-COVID-19 environment must focus on reforms to transition to a more resilient and efficient agricultural system through climate-smart agricultural solutions and mechanization. Combined with improvements in regional connectivity, such reforms will lead to higher value-added agricultural production that is better able to compete in regional and global markets.

52. Under the Plan, the focus will be on reforms that facilitate trade in agricultural products, including the promotion of e-commerce platforms and other digital technologies. The GMS Program will strengthen the biosecurity standards of countries by enhancing capacities in sanitary and phytosanitary (SPS) measures, which involve surveillance and inspection programs for plant and animal health, fisheries, food safety, and the management of processed foods. GMS countries will also be able to facilitate agreements on common regional SPS standards. Combined with appropriate biosecurity testing and tracking, this will reduce the time for clearance at border crossings. The GMS Program will work toward joint health and safety laboratory facilities at the borders. Significant efficiencies can be achieved through the adoption of common digital platforms for tracking produce and its biosecurity.

53. **Safe and seamless GMS tourism.** In 2019, the GMS received nearly 80 million international tourists that spent more than $100 billion in GMS destinations. Tourism contributed from 4.6% to 26.4% of GMS countries' GDP and employed millions of workers. COVID-19 has caused GMS countries to close their borders to international tourists, introduce domestic travel restrictions, and prohibit or curb access to tourist attractions.

Improved transport and trade facilitation. Thai government technicians conduct regular testing and evaluation of vegetables grown by farmers.

54. Mandatory quarantine requirements upon arrival in the GMS, and after returning home in some countries, along with safety and hygiene concerns also significantly suppress demand for travel. This caused GMS international tourist arrivals to fall by 70%–80% in 2020, and the industry may not recover to pre-pandemic levels until 2024. Widespread business closures and job losses have occurred across the entire tourism value chain, including among transport and accommodations providers, tour operators, restaurants, retail shops, and many other small and medium-sized enterprises. While domestic tourism spending is recovering and helping some businesses survive the crisis, it is unable to make up for the subregion's lost international tourism receipts.

55. The Plan will support GMS countries' coordinated tourism recovery efforts and initiatives to build back more resilient, sustainable, and inclusive tourism. This includes developing safe and seamless travel experiences that integrate digital technologies to facilitate reliable and rapid health screening at points of entry and at tourist attractions, adopting contactless payment systems, and introducing digital smart yellow cards to verify COVID-19 immunizations. Tourism destinations and businesses will implement government-endorsed health and safety protocols based on global best practices and develop harmonized regional safety standards and industry training programs for frontline tourism businesses.

56. The public and private sectors will cooperate to implement traditional media and digital campaigns that inform travelers of public health measures being undertaken and provide accurate, up-to-date travel information. Cost-effective digital marketing and promotion campaigns will leverage social media platforms and livestream tourist attractions using virtual reality to maintain GMS destination awareness among consumers worldwide. GMS governments will continue to provide aid and assistance to the sector given the significant shocks created by the pandemic, including social protection for unemployed tourism workers, tax and regulatory relief for tourism businesses, and liquidity to strategically important transport enterprises like airlines.

57. As outlined in the GMS Tourism Sector Strategy 2016–2025, GMS countries will develop green and resilient infrastructure in secondary destinations that are linked to subregional gateways. They will promote independent, self-driven, and small group holidays tailored to domestic and international market preferences. Collaboration between GMS countries' transport ministries and customs authorities will be critical to reestablish intraregional transport links and facilitate cross-border tourism, particularly to create proposed intraregional travel bubbles. GMS governments will also work together to promote flexible working arrangements and/or regional public nonworking holidays to stimulate domestic and subregional tourism demand, when the pandemic prevention and control policies permit, and circumstances allow.

VI. Implementing the COVID-19 Response and Recovery Plan

58.   The effectiveness of this COVID-19 Response and Recovery Plan is contingent upon strong coordination and collaboration among the national secretariats, the GMS Secretariat, GMS sector working groups and taskforces, and other key stakeholders of the GMS Program, including the private sector, local governments, development partners, and GMS knowledge centers. The GMS Senior Officials' Meetings will guide the Plan's implementation, with support from the GMS Secretariat, which will facilitate, coordinate, and report on the implementation's progress. The senior officials and the GMS Secretariat, will work with GMS countries, development partners, and the private sector to seek additional resources to implement the activities of the Plan.

59.   Coordinating and implementing the Plan's Pillar 1 – Protecting Lives, A One Health Approach will involve the GMS sector working groups on agriculture, environment, health, transport, and urban development. The health sector working group will lead the response on healthy people; the agriculture sector working group will lead in healthy animals, crops, and food products; and the urban development sector working group will lead on healthy city environments.

60.   Coordinating Pillar 2 – Protecting the Vulnerable and Poor will require the sector working group on health, the National Transport Facilitation Committee, and the proposed Task Force on Labor Migration.

61.   The implementation and coordination of Pillar 3 – Keeping Borders Open and Accelerating Inclusive Economic Activity will require the collective efforts of the sector working groups on agriculture, environment, health, urban,

Implementing the Plan. The effectiveness of the COVID-19 Response and Recovery Plan is contingent upon strong coordination and collaboration among key stakeholders of the GMS Program.

tourism, transport, and the National Transport Facilitation Committee. The National Transport Facilitation Committee will take the lead on improved transport and trade facilitation, the agriculture sector working group will lead in rebuilding agricultural trade, and the tourism sector working group will lead the implementation of safe and seamless GMS tourism.

62.   Some of the activities identified in each pillar will require actions that cut across sectoral working groups. Further, coordination across countries will be critical, particularly in areas where there needs to be common policies and regulations among immediate neighbors or throughout the GMS. The GMS Secretariat and relevant working group secretariats will act as coordination points where required. The GMS Economic Corridors Forum will also promote the development of border areas and economic corridors.

63.   Upon approval of the Plan, the GMS Secretariat will work with the relevant sector working groups to provide greater detail of the actions that will be undertaken and to identify those that will require intergovernmental support or cross-working group support. New plans prepared for each sector working group will incorporate elements of this Plan. Sector working groups will also coordinate with the Secretariat to prioritize the activities under the Plan that will have the greatest benefits across all GMS member countries. The GMS Secretariat will then convene for discussions across working groups as needed.

64.   **Priority Projects.** The Appendix contains an initial list of priority projects to support the Plan. The GMS Secretariat will expand and regularly update the list as new projects are identified—including projects financed by GMS countries or with the support of development partners—and will report on their implementation at the Senior Officials' Meeting.

APPENDIX
List of Projects Supporting the GMS COVID-19 Response and Recovery Plan, 2021–2023

DMC	Pillar	Project Name	ADB ($ million)	COF ($ million)	Source
CAM	1, 2	COVID-19 Active Response and Expenditure Support Program	250.00	241.57	ADB/JICA
CAM	2, 3	Community-Based Tourism COVID-19 Recovery Project	0.00	3.00	JFPR
CAM	1	Cambodia Rapid Immunization Support Project under the APVAX	95.00	0.00	ADB
CAM	3	Supporting Women Entrepreneurs to Prosper post COVID-19	0.60	0.00	ADB
CAM	1, 2	Greater Mekong Subregion Health Security Project (Additional Financing)	25.00	5.00	TBD
LAO	1, 2	Greater Mekong Subregion Health Security Project	20.00	0.00	ADB
LAO	1	Prevention and Control of COVID-19 Pandemic	0.00	7.50	US CDC
LAO	1	Lao PDR COVID-19 Response Project	0.00	18.00	IDA
LAO	1	COVID-19 Response Project	0.00	1.39	Japan UHC Fund
MYA	1, 2	Greater Mekong Subregion Health Security Project	30.00	0.00	ADB
MYA	1, 2	COVID-19 Active Response and Expenditure	250.00	0.00	ADB
REG	1, 2	Greater Mekong Subregion Health Security Project	125.00	0.00	ADB
REG	1, 3	GMS Sustainable Agriculture and Food Security Program	0.75	1.75	ADB/PRC PRRCF
REG	1, 2, 3	Policy Advice for COVID-19 Economic Recovery in Southeast Asia	5.00	0.00	ADB
REG	1	Strengthening Regional Health Cooperation in the Greater Mekong Subregion	0.50	0.50	ADB/RCIF
REG	1, 2	Support for Enhancing COVID-19 Vaccination Rollout and Expansion in Southeast Asia	5.00	0.00	ADB
REG	1, 2, 3	Sustaining the Gains of Regional Cooperation in the Greater Mekong Subregion	2.30	0.50	ADB/RCIF
REG	1, 2, 3	Implementing the GMS Strategic Framework 2030 for Supporting the COVID-19 Recovery	1.50	1.00	ADB/RCIF
THA	1, 2	COVID-19 Active Response and Expenditure	1.500.00	500.00	ADB/AIIB
VIE	1, 2	COVID-19 Relief for Women-Led Small and Medium-Sized Enterprises	0.00	5.00	Women Entrepreneurs Finance Initiative
		TOTALS	**2,310.65**	**785.21**	

Data as of July 2021.

ADB = Asian Development Bank, AIIB = Asian Infrastructure Investment Bank, CAM = Cambodia, COF = cofinancing, COVID-19 = coronavirus disease, GMS = Greater Mekong Subregion, JFPR = Japan Fund for Poverty Reduction, JICA = Japan International Cooperation Agency, LAO = Lao People's Democratic Republic, MYA = Myanmar, PRC PRRCF = People's Republic of China Poverty Reduction and Regional Cooperation Fund, RCIF = Regional Cooperation and Integration Fund, REG = regional as they are tagged as regional TA in ADB's system, THA = Thailand.
Source: Asian Development Bank.

www.ingramcontent.com/pod-product-compliance
Lightning Source LLC
Chambersburg PA
CBHW041122280326
41928CB00061B/3499